The Hospital Bedtime Story

Written By:
Jessica Ehret

Illustrated By:
Diane Lucas

Halo
PUBLISHING
INTERNATIONAL

ISBN: 978-1-61244-832-9
Library of Congress Control Number: 2020904011

Printed in the United States of America

Halo Publishing International
8000 W Interstate 10
Suite 600
San Antonio, Texas 78230
www.halopublishing.com
contact@halopublishing.com

To children and families who are
enduring a hospital stay;

May this book provide your child an opportunity
to relate, and ultimately, provide comfort at
bedtime, as they fall asleep in an unfamiliar
environment.

To the hardworking and compassionate
pediatric staff who acknowledge and support their
young patients' thoughts and feelings in *addition*
to their medical needs.

To the Child Life Specialists around the world
who are working to educate, prepare, and
support pediatric patients in playful ways-
helping children to develop the coping skills
necessary to face adversity.

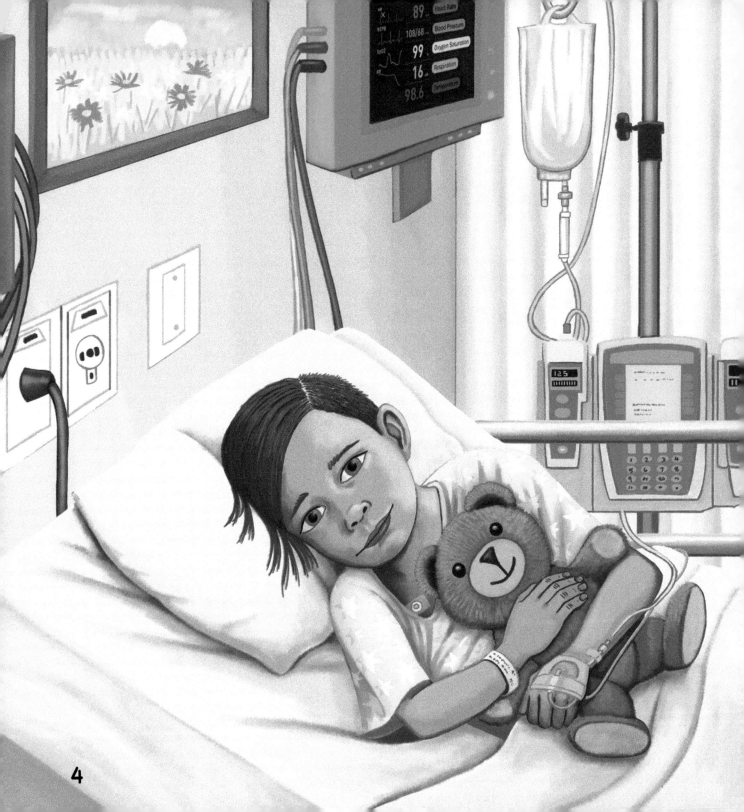

89 Heart Rate
108/68 Blood Pressure
99 Oxygen Saturation
16 Respiration
98.6 Temperature

4

Hello, my name is Riley!

Tonight I'm sleeping in a hospital bed,
but I'd rather be at home instead.

In this room, there are cords, switches, and screens
and lots of beeps from little machines.

Computers and stickers are monitoring me.
And my veins are getting a drink
through a tiny straw called an I.V.

The thermometer tickles across my forehead.
And the scale that weighs me is built into the bed.

The wrap around my finger measures my breathing.
It's always on, even when I'm sleeping.

There's whooshing and ticking, and sounds that go-- "PUFFFF!"
A tight squeeze on my arm from the blood pressure cuff.

My vital signs are checked regularly;
this tells us if my body is working properly.

I wonder how I will sleep with all this strange stuff around...
Who can sleep through all these unusual sounds?

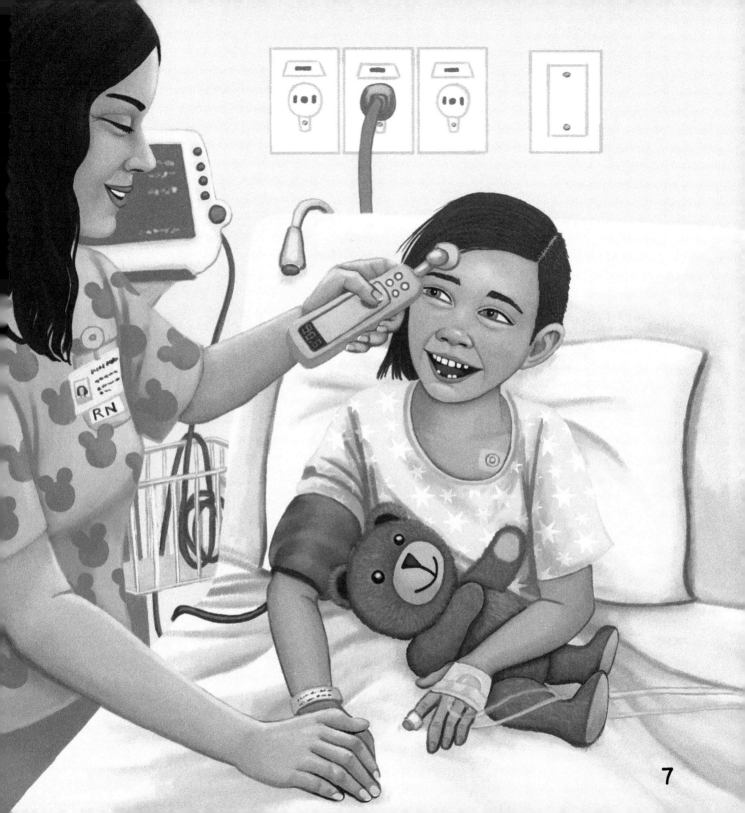

7

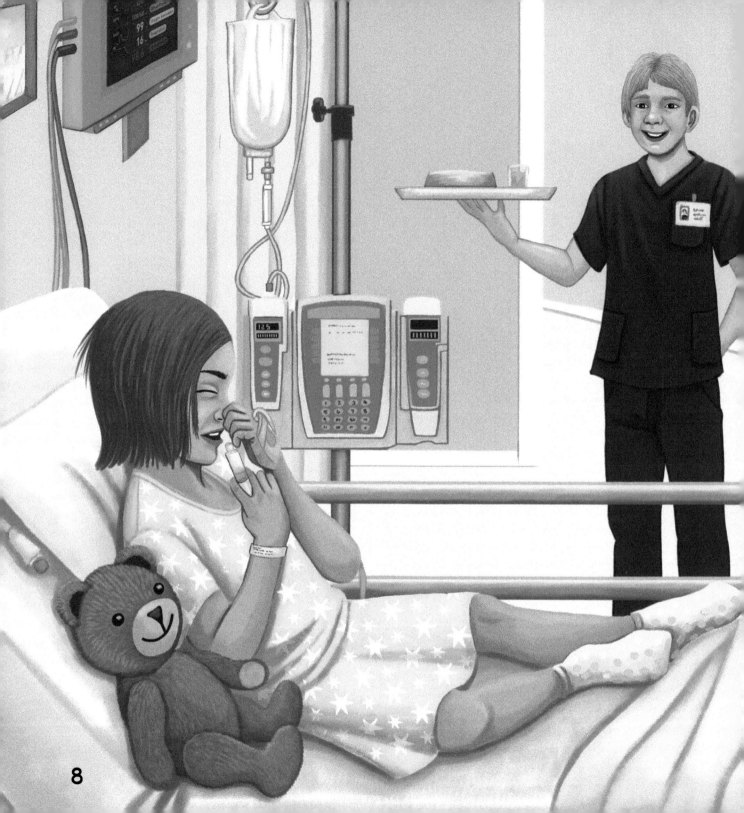

My name, age, and birth date are listed on my bracelet.
When I take medicine, I plug my nose so I don't have to taste it.

I'm wearing grippy socks and special P.J.s.
And when I get food, it's delivered to me on a tray.

If I need something all of a sudden,
I just push this red button.

On my window sill there's a gift basket and a bright balloon
with a card that says, "hugs and kisses, get well soon."

My routine was interrupted, so I'm not sure what to expect,
but staying flexible helps me get through whatever is next.

I don't have to worry about my unfinished chores,
my messy room, or possible test scores.

Any problems outside of right here, right now,
will work themselves out somehow.

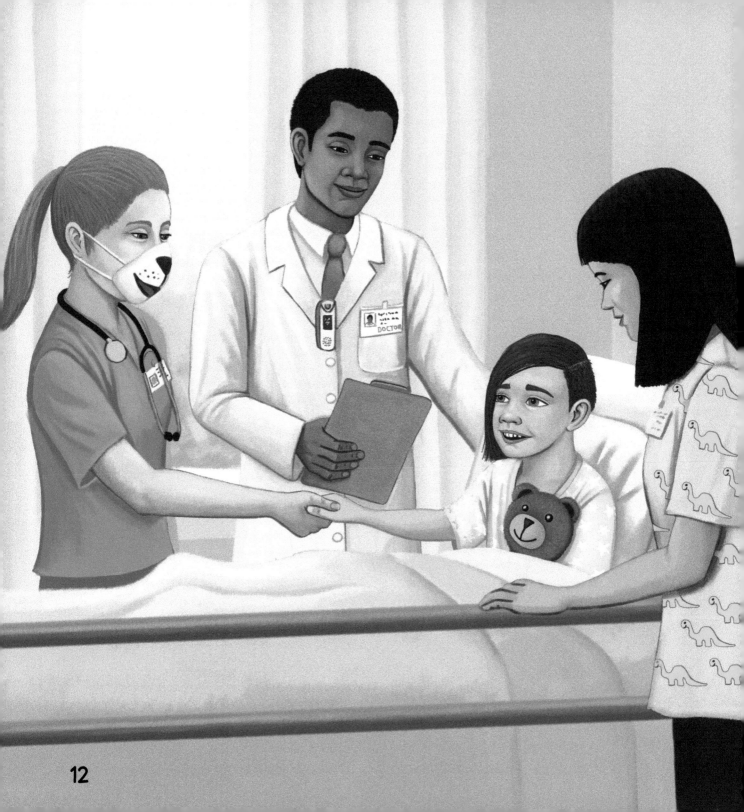

As I meet my doctors, nurses, and techs;
I'm sure to tell them all about me and what works best.

There's a whole medical team-
those are the people taking care of me.
They tell us that my health is their priority.

One of them is serious and has a lot of questions to ask.
One uses big words, and one wears a mask.

Out of all the hospital staff,
my favorites are the ones who make me laugh.

I've been taught to stay away from strangers,
but the people here are keeping me from danger.

I may not like some of the things they have to do,
but if it helps me to get well I will power through.

What I dislike the most,
is when I have to get a poke.

Holding still can be tricky,
but if I cooperate it goes quickly.

For some tests, there's no eating or drinking. I'm told I cannot.
For other tests, I have to drink and drink and drink a lot.

During procedures people tell me to stay calm,
even though I'm terrified.
They must not know how I'm feeling on the inside.

Luckily, a Child Life Specialist comes to prepare me beforehand.
They teach me and make sure that I understand.

Sometimes I'm scared, sometimes I'm strong;
I get upset, but it doesn't last long.
I'm reassured that I haven't done anything wrong.

I'm thankful to have family by my side.
They are my protectors and my guides.

They talk me through the toughest of times,
and reward my bravery with high fives.

It's helpful to know that I'm not alone;
there are other kids here-
some are babies, some are grown.

18

Toys, games, and crafts take my sad thoughts away.
It makes me happy to be able to play.
Maybe not like usual, but in a new way.

I pretend this isn't a boring hospital room.
It helps to erase the gloom.

I make-believe it's an art museum,
or perhaps, an ice cream shop, or coliseum.

My creations are hanging all over the place.
When people enter my room it brings a smile to their face.

All day long my ears have been listening;
my eyes have been watching,
and my body has done a lot of feeling.
I should get some rest now, so I can start healing.

Tonight, there are kids all over the world
who are going to sleep in the hospital;
just like me they are learning and doing things
they never thought possible.

As I lay here and look around,
I catch a glimpse of the sun going down.

It's quiet which is strange.
My door is not revolving,
and there are no intruders for a change.

In this moment I realize;
I am strong, I am loved, and I am happy to be alive.

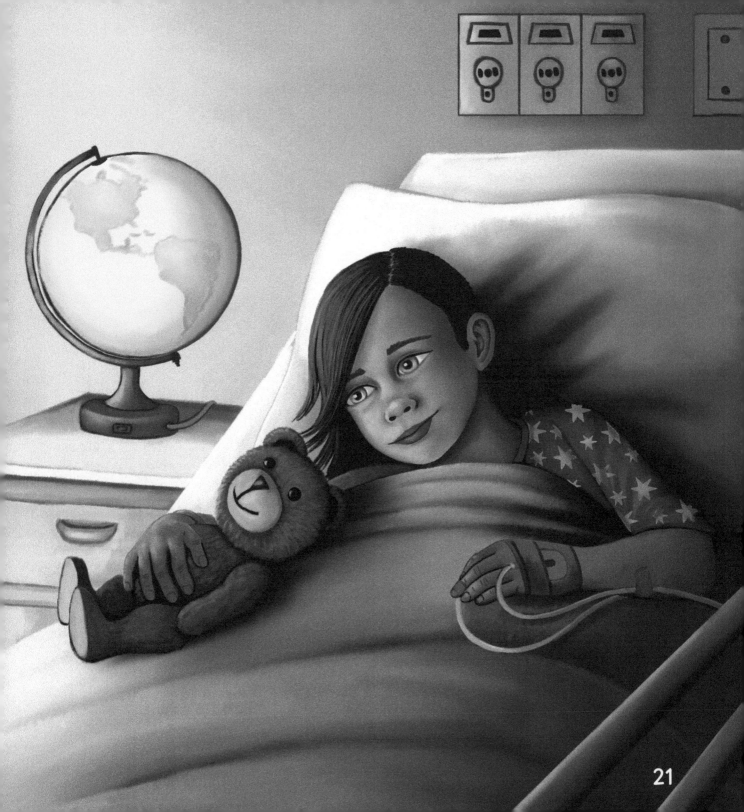

21

I take deep breaths to relax–
in through my nose out through my mouth.
I yawn, wiggle, and stretch my body all the way out.

It's time to turn down the light
and put my surroundings out of sight.

I place my hand over my heart to feel its pace.
I think happy thoughts of my favorite place.

I tell myself that everything will be okay
because tomorrow is a new day.

I'd rather be at home instead,
but tonight I'm sleeping in my hospital bed.

Printed in the USA
CPSIA information can be obtained
at www.ICGtesting.com
LVHW061645180524
780708LV00022B/305